SHOW ME! How to Draw Halloween

With this book, you can easily learn to draw Halloween characters and decorations that everyone loves. There are cute and various pictures waiting to be drawn with your pencil. By following the numbers in order, you'll soon see completed ghosts, vampires, and adorable little witches.

Drawing helps to spark your imagination and creativity, and also improves your focus. Don't give up if it's hard, just start with the easy drawings and soon your skills will get better. Once you've finished drawing, try coloring with your favorite colors too.

So, are you ready to grab a pencil and start? Let's begin!

PUMPKIN

① ② ③

④ ⑤

CUTE GHOST

①

②

③

④

⑤

DRAW YOUR PICTURE HERE

CUTE BAT

①

②

③

④

⑤

DRAW YOUR PICTURE HERE

TOMBSTONE

①

② ③

④ ⑤

DRAW YOUR PICTURE HERE

WITCH'S BROOM

①

②

③

④

⑤

DRAW YOUR PICTURE HERE

SPIDER

①

②

③

④

⑤

DRAW YOUR PICTURE HERE

WITCH'S CAULDRON

①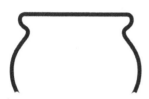

②

③

④

⑤

⑥

DRAW YOUR PICTURE HERE

FLYING GHOST

DRAW YOUR PICTURE HERE

WITCH'S BOOT

DRAW YOUR PICTURE HERE

FRANKENSTEIN

①

②

③

④

⑤

⑥

DRAW YOUR PICTURE HERE

WITCH'S HAT

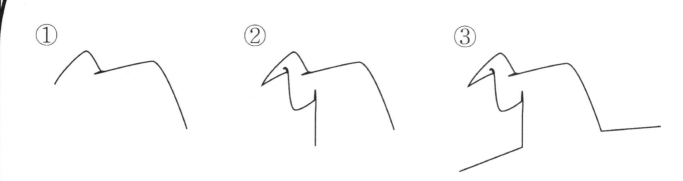

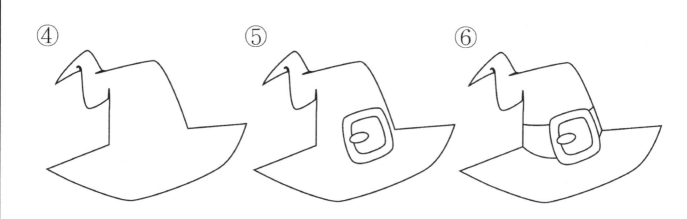

DRAW YOUR PICTURE HERE

CUTE WITCH FACE

①

②

③

④

⑤

⑥

DRAW YOUR PICTURE HERE

VAMPIRE

①

②

③

④

⑤

⑥

DRAW YOUR PICTURE HERE

JACK O LANTERN

①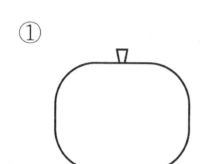

②

③

④

⑤

⑥

DRAW YOUR PICTURE HERE

OWL

DRAW YOUR PICTURE HERE

CUTE WITCH

① ② ③

④ ⑤ ⑥

SCARED CAT

①

②

③

④

⑤

⑥

DRAW YOUR PICTURE HERE

REAPER

DRAW YOUR PICTURE HERE

BIG EYE MONSTER

①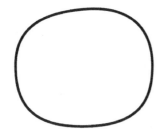

②

③

④

⑤

⑥

DRAW YOUR PICTURE HERE

PUMPKIN CANDY

①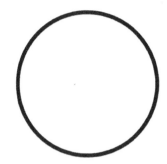

②

③

④

⑤

⑥

DRAW YOUR PICTURE HERE

WITCH'S CAT

①

②

③

④

⑤

⑥

DRAW YOUR PICTURE HERE

WEREWOLF

① ② ③ ④ ⑤ ⑥ ⑦ ⑧

DRAW YOUR PICTURE HERE

MUMMY

① ② ③

④ ⑤ ⑥

DRAW YOUR PICTURE HERE

FISHMAN MONSTER

①

②

③

④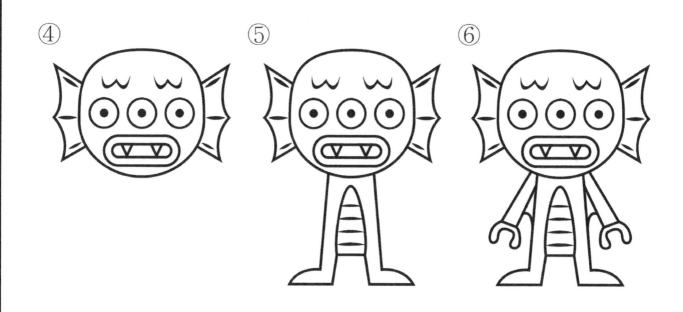

⑤

⑥

DRAW YOUR PICTURE HERE

SPIDER CUPCAKE

①

②

③

④

⑤

⑥

DRAW YOUR PICTURE HERE

CAT GIRL

①

②

③

④

⑤

⑥

DRAW YOUR PICTURE HERE

FLYING EYEBALL

① ② ③

④ ⑤ ⑥

DRAW YOUR PICTURE HERE

ZOMBIE

①

②

③

④

⑤

⑥

DRAW YOUR PICTURE HERE

HAIRY MONSTER

① ② ③

④ ⑤ ⑥

DRAW YOUR PICTURE HERE

ANGRY GHOST

DRAW YOUR PICTURE HERE

STRANGE EYED MONSTER

①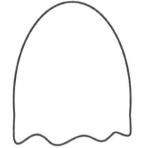

②

③

④

⑤

⑥

DRAW YOUR PICTURE HERE

MAGIC BOOK

① ②

③ ④ ⑤

⑥ ⑦ ⑧

DRAW YOUR PICTURE HERE

FLYING WHTCH

DRAW YOUR PICTURE HERE

SMILING PUMPKIN

① ②

③ ④ ⑤

⑥ ⑦ ⑧

DRAW YOUR PICTURE HERE

SPIKY MONSTER

DRAW YOUR PICTURE HERE

PUMPKIN MONSTER

①

②

③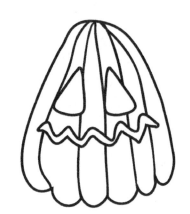

④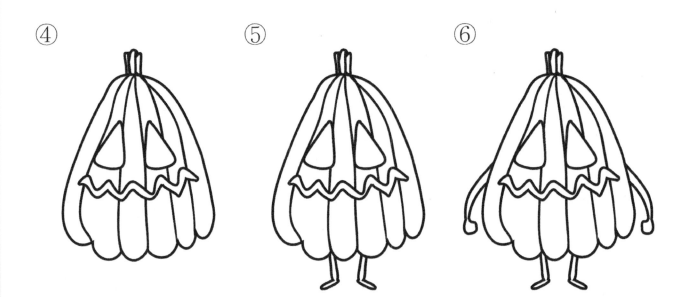

⑤

⑥

DRAW YOUR PICTURE HERE

DINO MONSTER

① ②

③ ④ ⑤

⑥ ⑦ ⑧

DRAW YOUR PICTURE HERE

6-ARMED MONSTER

① ②

③ ④ ⑤

⑥ ⑦ ⑧

DRAW YOUR PICTURE HERE

ZOMBIE HAND

① ② ③

④ ⑤ ⑥

DRAW YOUR PICTURE HERE

SMALL DEMON

DRAW YOUR PICTURE HERE

ONE EYED MONSTER

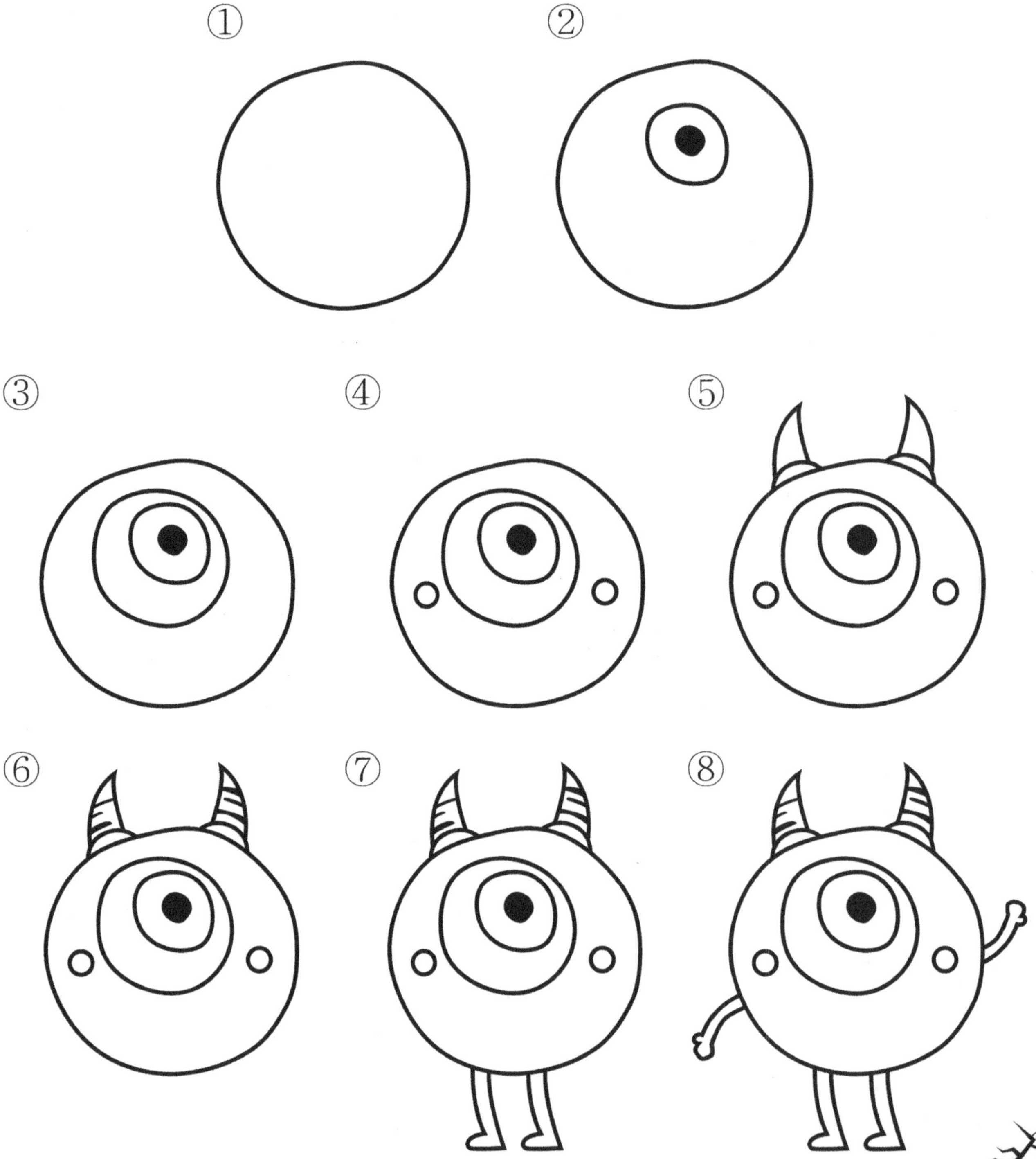

①

②

③

④

⑤

⑥

⑦

⑧

DRAW YOUR PICTURE HERE

CUTE VAMPIRE

① ② ③ ④ ⑤ ⑥ ⑦ ⑧

DRAW YOUR PICTURE HERE

GNOME

DRAW YOUR PICTURE HERE

SKELETON

①

②

③

④

⑤

⑥

DRAW YOUR PICTURE HERE

HAUNTED HOUSE

①

②

③

④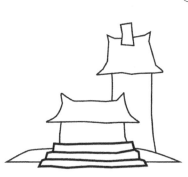

⑤

⑥

⑦

⑧

DRAW YOUR PICTURE HERE

ALIEN COSTUME

DRAW YOUR PICTURE HERE

PIRATE COSTUME

① ② ③ ④ ⑤ ⑥ ⑦ ⑧

DRAW YOUR PICTURE HERE

SCARECROW

① ② ③ ④ ⑤ ⑥ ⑦ ⑧

HALLOWEEN CANDY BAG

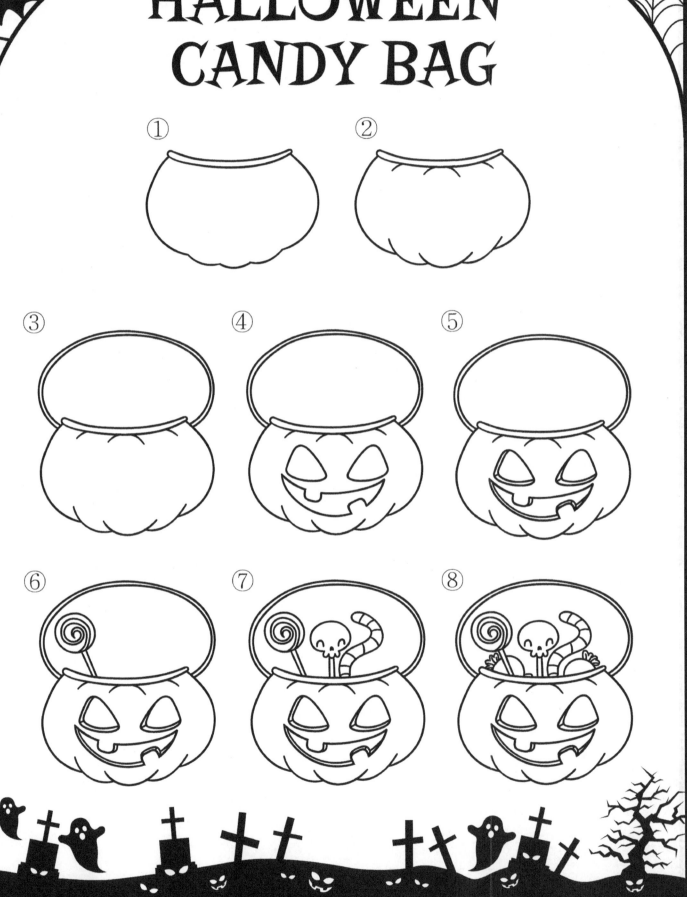

DRAW YOUR PICTURE HERE

ANGRY MONSTER

① ②

③ ④ ⑤

⑥ ⑦ ⑧

DRAW YOUR PICTURE HERE

Thank you for purchasing this book.
Check out other books from Followlight Books.

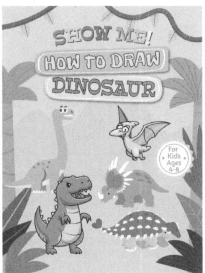

SCAN ME

Made in the USA
Las Vegas, NV
11 December 2024

13799077R00057